This collection, powerful in the linkages it draws between birth and sweeping change, will have you thinking about beginnings and foundations—and where you come from. In Cradles, birth is unsung labour and the under-acknowledged "gift ". It is also associated with a receptive space, a holding, a container in which hope and vibrancy can grow. After reading some of these poems, I was spurred to return to Maropeng—to touch again the rawness, starkness and wonder of earliest survival. On reading this, maybe you too will be inspired to explore again, in one way or another, something core, progressive and challenging about being human today.

> — Frank Meintjies, Johannesburg based poet,
> author of *My Rainbow* and *Unfettered Days*,
> and co-editor of *Voices of Transition*

Valiani in this collection gives credence to Wainaina's assertion that "… words must be concrete things. Surely they cannot be suggestions of things, vague pictures: scattered, shifting sensations?" Through her tangible words Valiani carries us from the often unmentioned and under-recognised cradles of our beginnings, through to those of the worlds we inhabit with varying levels of comfort with one other, and brings us full circle to the ultimate cradles of the cry of our souls, as they battle to find their own place in the world. She delivers this with the ease and the dexterity of both the aesthete and the ever so conscious activist. Cradles is a must read for everyone for whom words are an important facet of life.

> —Lindiwe Nkutha, Director of 'Joburg Rising'; author of *Rock* and other short stories.

Other works by Salimah Valiani

POETRY COLLECTIONS

breathing for breadth (TSAR: 2005)
Letter Out: Letter In (Inanna: 2009)
land of the sky (Inanna: 2016)

ESSAYS AND MEMOIR

A Shared Sea: Tsitsi Dangarembga and Zora Neale Hurston (www.brittlepaper.com)
The Girl Next Door, 14: An Anthology of Queer Art (www.brittlepaper.com)

RESEARCH MONOGRAPH

Rethinking Unequal Exchange: The Global Integration of Nursing Labour Markets (University of Toronto Press: 2012)

POLICY AND ACADEMIC PAPERS

https://utoronto.academia.edu/SalimahValiani/Papers

Cradles

New and Collected Poems

Salimah Valiani

Daraja Press
Montréal

Published by Daraja Press
http://darajapress.com

© Salimah Valliani 2017
All rights reserved.
Cover design: Catherine McDonnell
Cover photo (Ecuadorian Amazon): Prabha Khosla
Author photo: Sokari Ekine

Thanks to Beverly Little Thunder (Inanna Publications) and Gillian Sze (Gaspereau Press) for permission to cite previously published works. We have made every effort to obtain permission from other publishers whose texts have been cited in the text.

Library and Archives Canada Cataloguing in Publication
Valiani, Salimah, 1970-
[Poems. Selections]
Cradles : new and collected poems / Salimah Valiani.
Issued in print and electronic formats.
ISBN 978-0-9953474-9-6 (softcover).–ISBN 978-1-988832-00-5 (ebook) I. Title.

PS8643.A425A6 2017   C811'.6   C2017-902995-9

C2017-902997-5

For Colin, Nadia, Salah, and all that has passed too soon

Contents

Acknowledgments xi

Notes Verging on a Preface xii

WOMB

For Maleeah 5

Arousal 6

On labour 7

Theft 8

(untitled) 9

Wealth 10

Didar 2008 12

On Unity 14

Body Memory 18

(untitled) 19

On the Immaterial 20

Heart in Throat 21

Breathlessness 22

Mother 24

Tenderness 26

Heroes 27

On love XVIII 28

On love XIX 29

Sudan 2016 30

LAND(S)

Djemaa El-Fna, 2012   37

In search of language   39

On love XX   41

Offerings and convictions, National Action Day in Solidarity
with First Nations June 29 2007
42

Souvenir, Cape Town 2005   45

For Ottawa, [And all capital cities of the Christianised world]   46

love or death II   48

Land of the Sky   51

Marrakech   54

Climbing to Mandara, Kilimanjaro   56

Indonesia, 2002   57

Bwindi Impenetrable National Park   59

On love XXI   63

Forest Chorus   64

TIDES

For matoke stems and the graveless   69

Hand Washing Story of a Refugee Family   72

For Madrid [or, On the passage of 150 modern years]   74

Yen for the Americas   75

Camera after the storm [or, On collective memory]   76

La mesquinerie   77

On Disease   79

l'Autobus   82

Drifting, or: On industrialisation and deindustrialisation   84

Wooden Dream, Kampala 2007   85

On love XXII   86

Inequality 2005/2015   87

Ice in the lungs   88

Chains   89

breathless   90

WIND

silver and stones   97

Memorial of the King of Lukembe, 2013   101

Early Morning Train   104

Cartography of faith   106

Kalisthenics of Displacement   107

Circumventing Circumcisions   109

leap of hope   111

Wind   113

Toronto, 2004   114

Letter to us via Reetika Vazirani   115

On love XXIII   127

Last Note to a Brother-Comrade   129

Clifton Sunset   131

Bleeding Heart, or Toronto 2016   132

On Methodology   133

Closet Chant   135

Liberation   136

Acknowledgments

I acknowledge all that has inspired me, in the conscience and in the sub-conscience. I salute the art of the artists I have known and the art of those I never knew were artists. I applaud the lovers of art, the audiences we cannot exist without. I honour the ancestors, those that have died young, and mother earth that keeps rejuvenating us.

Notes Verging on a Preface

George Elliott Clarke

George Elliott Clarke is 7th Canadian Parliamentary Poet Laureate (2016-17)

Rare is that poet who can be sensible—even scientific—about the newsprint and banner-headline facts of liberation forestalled and revolution redacted, saints assassinated and lesser strivers bought-off and corrupted. Rare are those poets who can analyze political science when it is unmasked as police suppression or economics that is all about cons and comics. Rare are these bards, for poets tend to lean toward the sensual or the spiritual— or both, which is a way to seem apolitical or surreal—or both. But such a poet is not Salimah Valiani. A prize-winning economist (but no crank, unlike Ezra Pound), a scholar of labour and specifically of the caring professions, Valiani brings to her superb poetry a learned knowledge that all life is about labour—beginning with the labour that produces new human beings (and other beings) and ending with what is described as "laboured breathing." If Labour is the engine of existence, why should it be disdained and labourers repressed? Valiani attends this fundamental disjuncture—crisis—in our civilization. She knows that all Labour is akin to nursing, to nurturing: One labours over a poem; one nurses the poem along. Even th'erotic is about Labour—lovemaking (my emphasis), not to mention suckling, kissing, clasping, the sweat also of coupling. Or consider the domestic scene where spouse and child breathe and the onlooking spouse may "Swim in their breathing." Because Valiani understands that Labour is Love, Loving, and that which fosters the marvels of civilizations (note the plural), her poetry—loving Humanity and Nature—asks that we understand "Theft " as not only being a failure to redistribute 92 per cent of the lands of colonized South Africa, but that it is also that inequality that means pharmacists sell meds in locked cages (overseen by armed guards) and that pupils must carry their desks from class to class, for there are not enough to go around. Not only that, but what about the obscene observation that even flirting is feared by lesbians in the legalised homophobia of Uganda.

Poetasters who believe that poetry is only about aesthetics, about "Art for Art's Sake," may be read blissfully, for their words will never prod anyone to think, but only to sleep. Valiani comes to poetry as an activist who has not only studied oppression, but lived the reality of it—as the daughter of an exiled Ugandan and Tanzanian (of so-called 'Asian' descent), as a so-called "visible minority" person (just like me) in progressive, liberal, "tolerant" Canada, as a queer woman and parent amid societies where homophobia still dares bare its fangs, and as a woman—part of the 51% of the world's population who collectively own 1% of its wealth. So, Valiani reaches out; she claims kinship with Kwame Ture; she inks guerilla proverbs; she knows that Toronto is "African" and that Indigenous Canadians have much in common with Indigenous South Africans. Her collection wants to make whole—holy, really—the "whole of holes that is memory." Her poems are manifestos as valentines; sparks that represent "the igniting, going on, as we make a go of it".

Who does Valiani resemble? Dionne Brand, yes. But also consider Lizzie Borden—the director of Born in Flames (1983), that film so prophetic in its acknowledgment of the blunting of 1960s, radical insurgency. Consider also dedicated environmentalists, keen to preserve jungle, desert, and tundra. This is Valiani's passion too.

Brave is this poet and her poetry! She knows—like all true poets—that "Next to nobody / wants poetry." Right! Yet, there she is—here she is—delivering scathing insights, anyway, as in her lacerating, moving, unforgettable poem, "Letter to us via Reetika Vazirani."

Blessed Reader, you are not wrong. Not this time. These words—Valiani's— are the right words at the right time.

WOMB

Africa is the birthplace of humankind.
This is where our collective umbilical cord lies buried.

*

Life first emerged about 3.8 billion years ago.
Our journey begins in South Africa, where fossils of some of the earliest known life forms on Earth have been found.

— Entrance of the Cradle of Humankind, also known as Maropeng[1]

---

[1]. The Cradle of Humankind is one of humanity's places of origin situated in Maropeng, just outside of Johannesburg, South Africa. 'Maropeng' is a Setswana word meaning returning to the place of our origins.

Other mammals in the world have their babies and let them go. But we truly labour when we give birth, and when we give birth, it is a gift to our community. It is a gift to our people... Men aren't able to do that, so they have the piercing during Sundance. I'm told that when the skin tears away from that muscle, it's the equivalent of giving birth.

> — excerpt from *One Bead at a Time,* by Beverly Little Thunder (Toronto: Innana Publicatons, 2016)

For Maleeah

Your breathing to my breathing
lashes brushing neck
curls whisking ear
limbs wrapping
pulsing to pulsing

sensuous, precious

like the litchi juice you cling
4:19am.

Arousal

Though it has been
Over two years
You made me remember
Before even touching

Because you aroused me

Today's arousals
Recall yesterday's arousals
Weeding away
the moments in between.

On labour

Which labour
is most rarely spoken of?

the labour that makes women
capable of anything

the labour that breaks water
opens body parts
tears muscle, skin
and can't be insured for injury or harm

the labour that can last
two days straight
no breaks, no meals
no matter the collective agreement

Which labour talks
are side stepped
eluded
as though bypassing
can undo
this labour's
indispensability

The labour that produces
tears of an infant
tears of a mother

the labour from which
all life continues
or is sealed in the source.

Theft

In the ostrich farms of South Africa
Landless workers of ostrich farmers
(only some 8% of land has been redistributed)
Are directed to remove three or four ostrich eggs
from each new batch
Because the mother ostrich always replaces them
upon finding fewer eggs in her nest.

In the landless families of South Africa
The mother's ability to stretch herself
and provide for her husband (or his absence)
and provide for her children
and provide for her orphaned children
and provide for the elders
and provide for her children's children
Is seen as a sign of inferiority
rather than a sign
of historically engrained respect for responsibility.

minus another
love can still grow
(to unplanned and existing receptacles)

minus another
the thirsting can be replaced (possibly?) with
embraces in new places

minus another
the recalling of early months
gets stronger

minus another
those memories of the early
are more cherished, cradled
(less replaceable?)

minus another
the essential loneliness
laid bare for the gripping
like flailing limbs and stiff belly
of a newborn baby.

Wealth

Five sounds of 't'
Two sounds of 'k'
Four click sounds
How many sounds does your language make?

Twenty consonants, six vowels
Forty-five sounds
Four thousand characters...
Can we say,
the more letters, characters, sounds, gestures
the more richness and complexity
accommodated within?

Within what?
Within a language
a culture
a people
And the shared places of many peoples:
a metropolis
a nation
a world
a cosmos

Where do we meet
and how?
Who attempts first
to make unfamiliar sounds?

Do we meet at all
If not, why not?

Fifteen letters, twenty sounds, one thousand characters ……
How many worlds
does your tongue embrace?

Didar 2008

18,000 momins
52 different countries
multiple ethnicities
sparkling eyes
shining shoes (to be taken off)
kola zanana of people rebeginning

longing hearts
2,000 elders brought in on wheels and stretchers
6 rows
6 columns
36 quadrants
countless squares of white carpet
countless seva-hours of uncounting volunteers

3 days of pre-festivities
cones and cones of mehndi
kalio-paun
phul-kobi
butter chicken
bhaji
buses and parking
tasbih-making
candle-engraving
Kufic Art
Arabic calligraphy
countless seva-hours of uncounting volunteers

Les Couleurs d'Amour Art Gallery:
quotes of Hazrat Ali

symbols of Isa Nabi
Inuktuk enlaid with names of Allah
lion of East Africa
glasswork of Central Asia
mountains and light and love for the living

1 official welcome
5,000 unofficials welcoming
1 Grey Cup victory
18,000 momins chanting in
one breath of holy rhyming
18,000 momins silent
with a single drop of the eyelid
15 babies weeping
a two-year old missing
joyful 'loading zone' entry
(of anti-graffiti paint)
1 winding thin red carpet
1 modest stage
a sombre plea for collectivity
in poor economic times
a call against poverty
crossing generation lines
a whisper to seek
the language of plurality

1 living Imam
50 year link
in a chain of 49
1 Messenger
one sea of breathlessness
1 Love
the Unity of Allah.

On Unity

November 15, 1998
Dead today,
Stokely Carmichael
Kwame Ture,
What can I do for you today
This day
of your death?

Not until I saw one of the organizer's tags:
'Kwame Ture Memorial'
did it hit me,
your death
your 'transcendence to the ancestors'
as the Memorial Program said
your 'passing to the other side to join relatives in the spirit world'
as the first speaker, Native brother said
before recalling your solidarity at Wounded Knee
your presence at the occupation
of the Bureau of Indian Affairs
1973

What can we do for you
this day
of your death
Kwame Ture
But renew our struggling
as you kept-on renewing
Banned from one country
finding another country
Turned away at point of entry

trying again at another
Barred from entering
30 countries in total
including Trinidad and Tobago
your birth place
Banned from one place
finding another place
calling your callings
Always a calling
Black Power — Pan-Africanism — Pan-Socialism

Beginning on stage, a cowbell-melody recalling birth
and proceeding from back of the room
a deep drum-rhythm recounting the story of your life
Melody of birth and story of life
coming toward each other
and meeting at death
A West African praise-song to the dead
in memorial tribute to you
Kwame Ture
African Warrior
among several African Warriors
among several warriors
Bakule!
Bakule!

One thunderous applause
dedicated to you
Namibian-style
Instead of one moment of silence
Because your life was never about silence
Kwame Ture
though as Khafre Kambon said
you 'lived a life of poverty while raising millions for your party'
And you lived by these choices without words of complaint.

'One Unified Socialist Africa'
as you wrote at the end of each letter
at the end of the epitaph
you wrote for yourself, for us
Kwame
Dying in Africa
on the same principle upon which you chose to live there:
To share fully in Africa's sufferings
while working to alleviate them
As a child of Africa

With life constantly slipping through our fingers
and death everywhere
I know
today
Kwame Ture
It is exactly as Peter Tosh said
'Let the dead bury the dead
and who is to be fed, be fed'

Stokely Carmichael
Kwame Ture
'Two names
one leader
one friend'
as the Cuban solidarity message said
What can we do for you
this day
But keep on living
Each day to its fullest
'The revolutionary loves life'
Hugo Blanco said
'yet never flees from death and misery,
injustice
and hatred'

Pan-Africanism — Pan-Socialism
One living woman that I am
Kwame Ture
I'll help keep these dreams alive
Never growing impatient
because 'all impatience is selfishness and egotism'
as Kwame Nkrumah told you
in 1967
I will live by these dreams
help keep them alive
Until one day
I die
as you have now
Kwame
joining
countless others
leaving a spirit
of unity
behind.

Body Memory

—After *Belle*, directed by Amma Asante, written by Misan Sagay.

one year old leg crushing into abdomen
ribs crashing arm
How long is the body memory
Of the tight cushy-ness of the womb?

Is it short?

Short as the memory
that slave traders were once more powerful
than insurers

Short as the memory that the sale of people as slaves was
Abolished in parts of the thirteen colonies
before England

Or is it long

Like the memory of two African women today
Telling the unknown story of a female African aristocrat
in an eighteenth century English portrait.

Few know
think
imagine
to where the scent of a babe's head
may be traced

The scent of a babe's head
is a bud
of the scent
of the womb-blood
trailing
weeks and weeks
after baby's arrival.

On the Immaterial

She said
I can count on two
fingers
the times I've been lifted

He said
I don't remember
the number of times
I've been lifted
as a baby
small child
when ill.
But I know when I have felt held
skin to skin
tear drop to tear drop.

Today in Kenya
In the streets of Mexico
In South Korea
People are holding together
Because they feel unheld.

I can count on two fingers
the times I've been lifted
But today
with
My two fingers and
Entire being
I can and will
Hold.

Heart in Throat

The ripples burst to juice
Each time a wave crashes

The spoon suckles more
As the water comes to shore

The segments spray
like broken waves crashing rocks

The fruit quenches throat
like ocean quenches heart.

Breathlessness

A baby
Like fasting
Shows the path to humility

A baby is a means to
understanding
Mother
Grandmother
Wife
Self

A baby brings home
(even in the 21st century)
The 1918 midwife's thought:
Birth is not the miracle
The miracle is that newborns live

A baby reminds
Of all that could happen but shouldn't
And still does

A baby's voice
Is like the light
In a small part of the room
Cube of vividness
At sunrise

A baby's joy is
Whole
Yet unknowable
Unknowable yet fathomable

Breathtaking

Mother

When I was a child
I thought she was perfect,
my mother
I thought she was the world.
So when things went wrong
I thought it was cuz of her
If she was the perfect apple
and the world an apple of hers.

When I was a girl,
I bit into the apple
and saw the world inside.
There I saw my mother,
being what she was
A seed
of the core:
dark and smooth
not round and red,
oblong and peaked
as her teary juices said.

When I was a woman
I forgot about the seed,
tried to perfect and apple of my own
in the whirl of a world
where fruit is fucked with
and pruning is fruitless
cuz a bumper crop sells cheap—
My red shone

but I was alone
propping up the tree.

Now I am old,
I remember the seed
She is here with me,
she is me.
Oblong and peaked
Biting into life
Giving not pruning
Shedding skins
To build a core

Keeping it plain
in a waxy, shiny world.

Tenderness

a toddler places her hands
at her mother's heart and
falls asleep

an ageing warrior sings
'Kiss the war, I am still alive'

a Mozambican recalls for a younger Mozambican
'Before liberation, we couldn't even dream of a future'

female refugees
      in refugee camps in France/
      under promise of passage to Britain/
      fleeing Syria

   take contraceptives in anticipation of rape

one country where countless greetings yield a handful of waves
(usually from the same people)
another country where the greetings and gratitude received
surpass the greetings made

umfaz'obelede umfaz'owanyusela ngaphesheya komlonjana[1]

'We don't know how to die.
When we learn to die, we will learn to live and our war will end'
—a woman of Abya Yala

From Dr. Phumla G.-M.: Not forgiveness. Empathy and an ethic of care.

---

1. Translation from isiXhosa: a woman with a breast so long it fed those beyond the river

Heroes

On a plane
5 hours
Crammed in between
2 men
hanging over the arm rest
or my shoulder
I watch a film
about 2 men dying to be famous
lying for fame
to be loved by their sons
like they could never love their own fathers
(because he left too early or
beat his kids constantly).
The story is resolved
when 2 men stop lying
to their sons
(themselves)
And still find love
(of a lesser fame).

How do men speak to each other?

On love XVIII

dancing I make
love with the music
music my playmate

        my mid-dawn rescuer

singing
I speak with the music
music my sound board

        active listener
        microphone of pain

playing
I become the music
bass and treble scales
trill-stacatto-crescendo-decrescendo
accordion/piano

alone with the music
together with the music
dream longing reality
combed in one
wakefulness.

On love XIX

At night
for baby and lover
The things I do
are similar
Spoon their bodies
Nestle their bellies
Swim in their breathing
Pray for their fullest wakefulness.

Sudan 2016

—In dialogue with Hajooj Kuka's documentary,
Beats of the Antonov (2014).

the hope of hybridity

this is the hope of the future
(and story of the past)

The proof: *the girl song*
Sung from Blue Nile to
Nuba Mountains
suburbs of Khartoum

Songs of women in the everyday

> 'I am ill
> ailing
> No medicine can help
> Loving him is such a joy
>
> I am fainting
> Aching and fading
> no doctor can save me
> Loving him is such a joy'

> > They have the Antonovs[1]
> > We have the beats

---

1. Russian made airplanes used by the Sudanese state to drop bombs on so-called *others* - currently, especially, in Blue Nile and the Nuba Mountains.

No poet needed to write them
Anyone can make/play a drum

Everyone owns these songs

                                      They have the Antonovs
                                      We have the beats

Atwot, Amri ... Ingessana ... Nuba ... Zaghawi
The encyclopedia of ethnicities[2]
Everyone owns these songs

No more lullabies[3]
No more fake states[4]
Only girl songs

For all the Antonovs
petrodollars
fake states
The hybridity of histories:
sole hope for all.

---

2. Sudan was/is the most ethnically heterogeneous part of Africa composed of some 600 tribes. Globally Sudan compares to India which is composed of 1,652 different language families.
3. The title of a 1982 collection of poetry by Black Consciousness Movement leader Mafika Gwala. Black Consciousness as a liberation philosophy of the 1980s was likely the most embracing yet of South African hybridities.
4. In geopolitical terms, the state of 'South Sudan' was largely the creation of former South African president, Thabo Mbeki, built on an idealised notion of ethnic division as key to national cohesion. The USA created Serbia, Croatia and Bosnia along similar lines.

LAND(S)

250 million years ago, all the land masses that had risen from the seas joined together to form the super-continent Pangaea, which was surrounded by a gigantic ocean. It slowly broke apart to form the seven continents we know today.

—Inside the museum, Maropeng

The Himalayas, a massive 8 km high, 2,500 km long mountain chain,
formed within the past 30 million years,
after the Indian sub-continent slammed into Asia
due to the process of continental drift.

This cataclysmic event resulted in a number of environmental responses.
For instance, it brought about the monsoons in Asia,
which had a knock-on effect in parts of Africa
by drying out air currents and decreasing rainfall.

This and other global continental drifts caused the world,
and East Africa in particular, to become cooler and drier.
Expanding savannahs began replacing forests in East Africa,
and African animals, including the early primates that were our ancestors,
had to adapt to their new habitat.

—Inside the museum, Maropeng

Djemaa El-Fna, 2012

—For Salah

In Djemaa El-Fna[1]
You can climb winding stairs
to terraces in the stars
Or sit on patios
watching different
paces and gaits
acts and tricks
ancient, new, evolving, old

In Djemaa El-Fna
(in a dream)
I am re-meeting my mother
She is a student my age
in the anti-Apartheid struggle.
She tells me she is a student of learning
learning about learning
I tell her I am learning
about change and changing

In Djemaa El-Fna
There are those practicing
mastering their art
For 1,000 years
And those travelling a
caravanserai for
even longer

---

1. An age-old square in the age-old medina(city) of the age-old Marrakech.

In Djemaa El-Fna

        the cycle of faces
        the depth and length of change
        the timelessness of learning.

In search of language

What does it mean
that I learned the word angisakufuni[1]
Long before I learned
that nakupenda (in one of our languages)
may mean 'I love you' in one of your languages.

What does it mean
that in a dialect of internationalism
amidst plenty of Xhosa
I asked 'How can I extend
and be extended here'
And the answer I found was
'There is room here for overlap only in English.'

What does it mean
that in a place as unlike mine
as yours
I found so much familiar
Including the simultaneity
of total acceptance and total rejection.

In a Boer war museum exhibiting
confiscated weapons and jewelry
I read that incwadi[2]
can spell a complex message
of
white as love
pink as poverty

1. In Zulu, the ultimate expression of rejection.
2. A string of beads, in Zulu.

black as grief
green, feeling
yellow, wealth
blue, faithfulness
red as tears
striped, doubt
brown, disappointment
Is this mistaken
And if not
What
does it mean?

An old Ska song sings
'I take one look inside
and this is what I see
We need more love
We need more love in this community'
What does it mean
What does it mean
Yearning for understanding
What does it mean.

On love XX

Dai folk artists
of De-Hong prefecture
in Yu-Nan province
mix techniques:

                        chisel carving
                        engraving
                        gold plating

to turn 2,100 grams of silver into
a bride's adornment

In time
the work
is ready to be worn

In time the creation can adorn.

Offerings and convictions, National Action Day in Solidarity with First Nations June 29 2007

Today is a day we have seen coming
for many many years.

*

There should never have been poverty
for anyone in this land.

*

The Seven Wonders of Canada
revealed that Canadians are very affected
by the environment and its destruction
People in Canada today
are looking for restorative justice
holistic health
balance
They are learning from our teachings.

*

We need to build our healing path together
And we have begun today
here
on Victoria Island.

*

To all our First Nations brothers and sisters

and friends from across Canada
We welcome you to unsurrendered Algonquin land
Home of the Anishnaabe.

*

It is not an angry day
but we acknowledge the anger
with how we have been treated
in our own land.

*

A nation must come to grips with its history
both good and bad
To fully understand its identity.

*

We are not interested in retribution
but in reconciliation
So our people can heal and move on.

Many children did not survive the residential schools
Many elders will not live to see land claims settled
We must acknowledge our losses.

*

The first Native judge
was appointed to the Federal Court yesterday
We know that the first disappointment
Will be the first of many.

**

It is not about partisan politics
It is about clean drinking water.

*

Take your frustration and channel it for the better good.

*

Show the world you are here
And that you can make a difference.

*

Your words have the power to influence the actions of others.

*

Your own stories tell more and tell better
The injustice of First Nations
Better than any speech anyone can make.

**

We have waited 170 years as Anishnaabe
For our unceded land to be recognised
And we will keep waiting
We will be patient
Because we respect Canada
And we respect Canadians.

— excerpts from speeches of First Nations elders, June 29 2007, Ottawa, Canada.

Souvenir, Cape Town 2005

The things I thought I'd miss,
I merely remember:

fruits of the land and sea
(small and succulent)
the seasons
(all four, like Spring and Summer in the different parts of another home)
the wine
(the only thing costing less than the average wage)
the oceans.

The one souvenir:
dancing to Vul'indlela
with a Kenyan
in African Toronto.

For Ottawa, [And all capital cities of the Christianised world]

—Inspired by Alana Levindosky and Colin Linden

his notes were round, red
to stretch the mouth around

her voice was wide, cracking
raw to one side
high and thin to another
nasal, raunchy to another

her strumming trembled
like her thin back

his guitars were slender,
voluptuous,
natural, synthetic
all bouncing through
every molecule in the room

her stories were rooted in
schizophrenia, Jesus, danger
her lyrics, unexpected, inconsistent, full
like prairie open truth

his black hat
and orange-embroidered-lapel-flower
were warm
as the raspy breath between notes

warm as his memories of the old souls of the blues
warm like her parallel
between doing cover songs and phoning far-off friends

    if they could speak
    the secrets of Ottawa would sound like this

love or death II

A small being
bent over tulips
A small being
draped over a bed of tulips
A small being blending with a turban of tulips
capping a piece of ground.

Is she smelling their scent
Is she bowing to their wealth of colour
Is she spilling tears in their thirst

When she delves into them
What they cannot speak, she can smell
What she cannot grasp, they can drink
Her breathing so much closer to her senses
when she delves into them
But like drinking becomes choking
when the swallowing becomes swilling
the tulips open up
only in the end:
when their falling petals
peel away all possibility of depth
So close to these tulips
yet always so far away
Her desire for depth, an idea
but the tulips, beings of their own
Like the double-samara of the maple tree:
yellow-green, two-seeded, winged-fruit
flying and falling from the maple tree
before the coming of the maple leaf

Slight, evanescent wings
she can clench in her palms and smell
only until they wilt and slip
through the cracks between fingers
Like the sight and scent
of the March 21st henna[1]
on her bloodless hands:
first laying themselves in her,
brightening fragrance
lightening
then fading
Like rhododendrons
in late May:
always blooming,
always a short season
Spring
and its bringing
of new freshness which ripens quickly
Spring
a beginning
thus always evoking an end.

*

A small being bent over tulips
A small being draped over a bed of tulips
A small being blending
with a turban of tulips capping a piece of the ground—
She is longing for intensity
which will deepen over a period
rather than pass like a season
She is longing for intensity
which will deepen over a period

---

1. The Spring equinox of the Northern hemisphere marks the Persian New Year, celebrated by many beyond Persia, for some with henna.

Like the moisture of rainwater mixed with sweat from walking
makes her smell of herself all the more
She is longing to place her scent
in the smelling of something changing
from one state to another state to another
rather than smelling a new thing each time
She is longing for immersion
Like the way she merges with breath when swimming:
something she can hear
     as it dips itself into water
something she can count
     —its beat—
     with the bubbles it blows,
something she can almost see
     like shimmering ripples of water
     yet never catch
     because of its indefinite
ceaselessness
     and her interminable oneness with it

She is longing for the ground:
to weave and be woven
Like veins within the crust of the earth.

Land of the Sky

days like this
I see you
eyes etched in rock
steady
Telling
That everything changes
and nothing changes
Buddha's balance
The weight of the Rockies
4,000 year old goddess
stones of the earth
we are
of a breathing
caked
in layers of plates
shifting inch-by-inch

                    nights like this
                    your giant paintbrush strokes
                    white light
                    rugged
                    on dark-grey-blue
                    I stop asking
                    what you are
                    Lose sight of
                    what we are
                    one eye light
                    one eye dark
                    at a place where

                knowing
                falls away

days like this
your rich solid ridges
flushing further and further West
from plush hills rolling East
Remind that
nothing arises from nothing
every growth, every movement
may give rise to another
that history moves in cycles
that the tendency is
circular

                nights like this
                your twilight
                      cloudlight
                your broad midnight blue

                    days like this
                  I know you are here
                    Even if
                    I can't see you
                    can't trace you
              can't show you to others
                    I feel your
                      encasing
                  in the thick mist
              Feel your presence in
              the smell of the air
          your reach within its coolness

                    days like this
                  I see you up close

rock rippling high
beard of cloud
evergreen skirt
with beetle-tinged orange
your shadowy valleys
pencil-thin lines
of your many etched faces

days like this I see you inside
your evergreen skirt is
multi-leaf, multi-green
your beard of cloud is
your sudden grey afro
your height is your steepness
your pencil-thin lines:
thigh-wide roots
woven over
150 million unfathomable years
your sage green floss
your sun-lime moss
your lime green mould
charcoal chiselled in ash
your tawny brown patches
are your many etched faces
one of the many that are one.

Marrakech

In the desert
the air is thinly dry
but because of the heat
the skin is velvety-supple

In the dark streets of the medina[1]
covered and three steps wide
the doors, two steps high
lead into
a tiled world of mustard gold, blues, greens and cream
courtyards incandescent by open sky

The broad Gileez[2] streets
of art deco pink
yellows and beige
sell more wine than
mint tea
but as in the medina
the mix of cafés,
coiffures, glaciers
is the same

In the desert as in
any other place
you can spot open
scraggy spaces
and crinkled plastic bags
mauve, blue, pale

1. The old city.
2. The new city.

What you see next are the
shacks of the shanties
In the desert
as in any other place.

Climbing to Mandara, Kilimanjaro

slow rising
sole standing
touch of smoothness
touch of coarseness
fire of flowers in the rainforest

half an unripe berry for one
half an unripe berry for another
ten thousand raindrops
tapping ten thousand leaves
warmth of a dry kanga
like clouds nestling a peak

ancient mahogany uprooted
hartlaub turaco: dark until it spreads its wings
things come apart when we try to put form to formlessness

if I am a tree
climbing a tree to reach the sun
do your roots sink
beyond these mountain trails

Indonesia, 2002

smell of tin
in monsoon heat

shanties of Jogja
only learned of after

Bollywood songs on guitar
and dogs at Kuta Beach

whole squid full of roe
obediently chewed in Lampung

flying hills of an ojek[1]
between Mataram and Sengigi

hot sex stolen in hidden places

three shades of blue
separating Gili Trawangan and Lombok

Buddhist-Muslim inn keeper in Gili
just surviving the bombings in Bali

resplendent elephant races
in a field after Mataram, before Surakarta

Wonokromo of colonial Jawa
where Nyai Ontosoroh rose from nothing
with the help of a Dutch man

---

1. Unregulated and most reasonably priced form of collective transport in Indonesia.

and was later fallen
by the family of the Dutch man[2]

innocent coral
of still unmined beaches.

---

[2]. Nyai Ontosoroh is a protagonist of *The Buru Quartet*, a series of historical novels written in the Buru prison by Pramoedya Ananta Toer, political prisoner of the Suharto regime.

Bwindi Impenetrable National Park

— To the park workers of Uganda

How to know
the road
Of the rainforest?

By the thickness
or thin-ness
of trees?
By the yellow mould
on stones
Orange mould on stones
Tawny-orange mould on tree trunks?
By the patches of nibbling ants?
surprise plots of wild apples
meandering blue flowers
By the creeping miniscule ferns
carefully examining forest floor —

                    *

No matter the angle
I can't capture
The depth
of this
Impenetrable forest

Can't capture the vast
                        profusion of trees

                                        shrubs
                                                shrubs with flowers
                        vines— green and red
                                        dripping

Can't escape the shock of
                sudden empty spaces
                where sky breathes light into
                the midsts

Can't fathom the relief
                        of the many shades of green-yellow
                                spicing branches and rays.

                *

        When I ask
        in the forest
        on the mountain
        (or in the savannah)
        What is this/
                What is that?

        What I am asking
        And what you give
        along with the *name*
        Is the story used by humans (from ancestral times to present)
        To try and understand what is essentially
        Humanly
                        Unknowable

In this name-giving
Through this sharing
one vulnerable human being to another
Travelling together a rainforest in search of *engaj*[1]

                                        *(mazike)*²
                                        *(mountain gorilla)*³

of the *Rushengura Group*

We arrive at a place

where a cousin-being sits
        back against tree
        peeling layers of bamboo
        tasting the crunchy tears inside

where a cousin-being gropes a trunk
        climbing up and away
                for a sigh of solitude

where a small engaj lifts a smaller engaj
                and moves away from what is feared

We arrive at a place

                Where
                'roads'
                'capturing'
                'penetrating'
                (words)
                lose meaning

        And what remains
          What exists
Is the depth of the here and now

                now hunger

---

1. The Rukiga word used to refer to the large dark mammals of the Bwindi forest. Rukiga is the language of the locale in which the mountain gorilla live.
2. The Luganda word used to refer to the large dark mammals of the Bwindi forest. Luganda is a widely-spoken language in Uganda.
3. English word used to refer to the large dark mammals of the Bwindi forest. English is another widely-spoken language in Uganda.

now joy
now solitude
now fear

On love XXI

earth
fire red
burning the ground

fire flowers
scraping sky
scorching clouds

rooibos steeped in rosy dawn

river reeds blowing songs

soup of rainmaking
wrap my heart

cool the ecocide
cool the ecocide

Forest Chorus

A musician told me
the most amazing thing about the Amazon
is the thick
constant
chorus of sound

    *

In the depth of Bwindi
I listened for the sound
but it was not as thick
as the rainforest
which drowned it out

    *

at Kibale
without listening
I heard
the thick
chorus of sound.

TIDES

On a hot day in Yongchun,
a girl is sent out to collect bitter leaves for dinner,
and in her chore, is suddenly graced divine.
.
.
.
The instant she hits water, she splits in two.
Just cleaves at the waist.
Her upper half flows north
(one may even call it America)
her lower half flows south.

Amidst the haze, a fisherman farther along shore
would've mistaken her for a catfish,
an inky glint, resolute and out of reach.

— excerpt from 'The Tale of Dark-Face Sze, Fujian, 1400 years ago',
in *Peeling Rambutan,* by Gillian Sze (Kentville: Gaspereau Press, 2014)

Australopithecus alarensis individuals
—one small, the other bigger—
walking side by side, left their footprints in wet ash
after the nearby Sadiman Volcano erupted.
Soon afterwards Sadiman blew again,
leaving a second layer of ash to
seal the footprints until they were discovered
and excavated in the 1970s.

*

1.9 million years ago homo ergaster moves out of Africa into Europe and Asia.

— Inside the museum, Maropeng

For matoke stems and the graveless

— To Mary Karooro Okurut, whose novel, *The Invisible Weevil*
helped me to understand.

I don't know
what it means
the word
dislocation

I do know
how it feels
to return to a place
birthplace of your mother
(after 36 years)
and find gaping
holes
in walls remembered
   doors remembered
     homes and roads remembered

Gaping holes of memory

I do know
how it
feels
To search a school

for signs
of what once was
And find only
empty classrooms
empty laboratories
dust
and a few blue desks
    (carried by students
    class to class
    because there just aren't
    enough anymore)

I know how it feels
to look for graves of the dead

                  4 Aunts
                        a Grandfather
    never met
    but known
    spoken of
    cherished all your life

And not find them in
the cemetery where they were
left

The whole of holes that is memory

I know
now
the feeling
of those who remained

    became different victims
    of the same dictatorship

Those who buried matoke stems
    (sacred source of
    a staple food)
    instead of
    unreturned
    bodies
    of the dead

Now I know
the feeling

of dislocation and the feeling

of dislocation without dislocation.

Hand Washing Story of a Refugee Family

what happens when you go
to your maami[1] dying
in a faraway hospital?

you learn the 7 steps
of washing hands:

rinse to lift
the dirt inlaid
(the wrong you did her
not visiting when she was healthy)

lather on soap
soak up the guilt

rub the fingers between each other
palm-to-palm
(reconnect with long lost cousin brothers and sisters
your maami's daughters and sons)

flip one hand over
rub fingers through fingers again
palm to back of hand
(meet your nieces and nephews
maami's children's children)

circle each palm
with fingertips of other hand
(ask your maami questions
that can undo historic tensions)

---

1. Gujarati and Kachhi word meaning wife of mother's brother.

rub each thumb
inside wrapped fingers
of the other hand

think of how not to repeat this

rinse and dry
say goodbye
fly away
So long/Wereba.²

---

2. Luganda for goodbye.

For Madrid [or, On the passage of 150 modern years]

The gnarly but comely
chandelier of 1750
With its 18 flames
and two surrounding mantlepieces
(sculpted brass and ebony
symbolising the three seasons: wheat, grapes and birds)

asked

The Palacio de Comunicaciones (1909)
stretched over the angles of
Paseo del Prado/Paseo de Recoletos/Caille de Alcala'

'But aren't you lonely?'

The Palacio replied

'How can I be lonely in this city of art
Surrounded by earth
air
fire
and ether
Sending letters to the world.'

Yen for the Americas

Wandering
he found
sound:
hands meeting a drum,
crickets meeting city-night,
waters rush-rush-shing together
at the tip of a piece of land:
memorial park commemorating war and trade
memorial park built atop someone else's burial ground.
Opening
he began to listen
at the tip
of a piece of land
jutting into a place
where two rivers meet.

Camera after the storm [or, On collective memory]

It was some time before
the film was developed
Because the memories were not yet ready
to be faced in full colour.

La mesquinerie

tu me dis
sois dans le futur
pas dans le passé
comme s'ils n'étaient
pas reliés

        l'avarice

sois généreux
arrête de nier
les yeux qui ne regardent pas
n'ont rien
à donner

        la mediocrité

Ben Jelloun dit:
"Rien de la verité ne m'est
epargné. C'est le besoin de parler
pour ne pas étouffer"[1]

        la crainte

Tagore dit:
"Le poison est un feu
dans lequel il faut se brûler
afin de pouvoir
recommencer"[2]

---

1. Tahar Ben Jelloun, 2007, *Les Pierres du Temps,* "Le retour de Moha," p. 85 (Paris: Editions du Seuil).
2. Rabindranath Tagore, 1985, *Gitali,* p. 43. Traduction (de bengali à l'anglais),

la mesquinerie ou l'honneteté
le futur ou le passé
choix artificiels
paix forcée.

Brother James (Dhaka: The University Press). Traduction en français, Salimah Valiani.

On Disease

Bumpy
white
wire
plastic
strip lock

                a cage

                Inside
                drugs
                to cure.[1]

This was the norm
before
in another era
here

                in this nation
                of particular
                inequality

But the cage was
stretched open
by collectives
inside/
worldwide

---

1. In South African pharmacies, medication is ordered, priced and packaged at the pharmacist counter. Customers then carry the medication, in a locked white cage, to the cashier and pay for it. Then the cage is unlocked. For further 'protection', there is a censor-alarm at the pharmacy door and an armed guard.

which saw
then learned

                        the cage

Taught others
to see and know

This exposure
was the first pry
open.

Still, it could have been different.

The entire shop
of cages

                        the rows
                        shelves
                        tills
                        straight jackets

could've been
dismantled

Then the boxes
bottles
jars and
salves
would've transformed

                                              many ceasing to exist.

*

Some wires
were pried open

                        The shop
                        the cages
                        the lock
                        remain.

l'Autobus

Elle avait peur
de tomber
Sur les roches pointues
fixées dans la rue,
une fois
des cailloux
éparpillés par terre.

Elle s'inquiétait,
elle se demandait:
Quelle roche était-elle?
quelle roche était sa mère?
quelle roche, son grand-père?
Autrefois
—soit-disant—
des cailloux libres
roulants dans le vent.

De l'émotion à la réflexion
Les moteurs se rechargent
et le feu change
Un autobus approche
lourd sur les roches,
écrasant les cailloux

Elle monte dans l'autobus,
elle absorbe sa largesse
et se libère de la lourdeur par dessous
Elle étend son bras

à sa mère
à son grand-père

Dans l'autobus les générations se traversent.

Drifting, or: On industrialisation and deindustrialisation

With the intensification of war in the early 1940s
Chinese of British Columbia
no longer sent bones home to China
(bones of expired miners, builders, cooks...
Because there were no boats to spare.

Are the ghosts of the Lebreton Flats
(environmental toxins drifting through Chinatown Ottawa in 2005)
remnants of the same Industrialising Age
similar or different
to the displaced bones of Chinese-Canadian workers?

Is the disorientation caused
by environmental toxins
similar or different
to the disorienting nature of unstable jobs
killer working conditions
weighty head tax debt?

Waves of exclusion
early 20th century
early 21st

Wooden Dream, Kampala 2007

67
dazzling smiles
snuck in
interchanged
each morning
for 8 days

a favour
a generous tip
by her
for her
if and when
the opportunity
arose

1 dream catcher
2 wooden earrings
in parting.

chance path-crossing
writer
waitress
grafted in
separate trajectories
miscarried
by love
outlawed.

On love XXII

—for Mondrian

some memories deepen

some become more pronounced

some memories layer
inlaying tiers of emotion

some memories blur
melding edges of emotion

some memories thicken
as the mind's pen forgets to
stop sketching loss

some memories curl
like time's retreat to recall

some memories leap out
trying
unsuccessfully
to fill the gap

some memories age
in a jug called Love.

Inequality 2005/2015

is it sewage
dampness
the smell of toilets in South African suburbs?

are these
traces
of something more
A bigger chasm?

ten years later
then in Cape Town
now in Jozi
this body memory
Shakes me back.

Ice in the lungs

whiskey-fuelled breathing

domed plastic vases of artificial flowers
laced with high Xhosa voices and compelling baritones

the giddy descent, swift unraveling of denouement

Ice in the lungs
the politics of learning
fear
sex
honey, sunlight, dew

Ice in the lungs
1976 South Africa
and mere survival.

    —Meditation on Gerald Kraak's crushing novel, *Ice in the Lungs*.

Chains

Ma gave an ocean to all,
Daughter swam an ocean
learned its roads
followed its weeds
met its creatures
made a home of open doors there
Sister sang a ship into existence
and whistled its horn from coast to coast to coast
Little sister danced herself into an undercurrent
and watched the way things moved around up above
Auntie wished for wells for people to drink from
and charged a small fee, hidden below
Niece chose to be a ladle
because she liked dipping in
and sharing what she found
Grandma swallowed snow when it came down hard
Grand-daughter flooded spaces into ice rinks,
showing how to skate with the cold
Cousin-sister built mills to generate electricity from the wind
Her cousin-sister used her own breath to try and warm the wind
full of chills

Histories are chains
in which we are links
To rub on them and tug them
toward another twist
Or be wrapped up
in rusting imbroglio.

breathless

Without knowing it
I left all that I knew
9 years ago
I've been here searching
then waiting
4 years each
My arms are branches
My chest of acacia twigs and leaves clotted together
My head has been emptied
And has grown back again.

In the desert
of so much of some things
and so little of others
One can learn patience.
With this patience
one can find the knowledge
of one's own rhythm
and the restfulness to swerve
when one's rhythm swerves

The knowledge of this rhythm:
Locating where one's past ends
and the present takes over
Conceiving of the 'organic categories'
of the Great Digest of Confucius
To attain 'precise verbal definitions of one's inarticulate thoughts'

The beat of this rhythm
is the anonymous art of the heart.

I am waiting in this desert
fasting in caves,
travelling parallel to caravans,
beating with this art
I am waiting in open flatness
for contour, as I once had
now substance which I understand.

There have been storms in this desert.
Battles and battlegrounds
Killings and murder
A liberation fighter bound up
and made to sing the anthem of another people
Dormant bombs dropped from low altitudes
to be activated by bouncing balls,
by the hoes of peasants
An advocate ordered to un-advocate
on national TV
A town's sewage dug up,
mixed with industrial waste
and placed at the front door,
alongside the town's water supply
A manufactured hailstorm
tearing away the olive harvest

A sandstorm can last five hours.
The choice is to move and keep moving
Or be locked in by sand
which builds around anything stationary.
To begin a journey in a sandstorm is good luck
says the old joke (full of heavy truth)
of the Zwaya and Majabra tribes
Battles can be long but can't last forever
The engaged traveller gains in the luck
of learning the hard way.

In peace as in war
there is risk.
In the face of risk are eyes of mystery
The mystery of unknown terrains
The mystery of what human beings can do to each other
and to those that are different from them
The mystery of what human beings can withstand
The mystery of a face which has never locked eyes with another

My neck has been drawn to the face of risk
My breath sucked in to its eyes of mystery
Intrigue is like a drug
and inquiry, a trip
which usually ends
Often in falling.

In the desert there can also be the silence
of not speaking to a soul
for one day and two days
The mystery of extreme sensitivity:
being able to sniff
a lone scent in the distance
The mystery of the tranquility
of breathing in the lungs of one's own soul.
Can anyone else be found here?

My arms are branches
My chest of acacia twigs and leaves clotted together
I am dead but can still be made love to
Dead but still can be burnt to death
I am dead but I can still fly to strange and familiar places
I am dead.
Please don't be the thing
that kills me again.

WIND

As they exited the walls of Mapungubwe Marubini, Chenayi and Chata were all seized by mitshimbilo, the disease of the wanderers. Perhaps they would settle for a while at Chata's mine in the land of the Karanga. Or perhaps they would follow the songs of the insects and the grass to the fabulous new town of the zimbabwes further north.

One never knew with mitshimbilo.

—excerpt from *The Sculptors of Mapungubwe*, by Zakes Mda (Cape Town: Kwela Books, 2013)

Sometimes the continents slide past one another, sometimes away from one another and sometimes they collide. Dramatic natural phenomena result when the continents move —earthquakes, volcanoes, tsunamis, and the creation and destruction of mountain and oceanic trenches.

—Inside the museum, Maropeng

silver and stones

young girls and boys in Mathare[1]
enjoying a game of soccer
with a ragged ball made
of plastic bags and string

a toddler lounging on a pile
of what happens to be garbage

a young retiree
looking forward to Chinese take-out
because the treatment for his cancer
doesn't let him keep down anything else

favelados dancing, drinking pinga[2]
to celebrate the end
of another year of life

waves of Asian labour
(each replacing the former, the former now 'too costly')
and the gleaming work songs
that the people bring with them

>   In one arc of the wheel there is stunning beauty
>   In another arc there is always
>   only the bareness of being

I opened a poem
and like a gull flying from a magician's hand
there came a song:

---

1. A large slum of Nairobi, Kenya.
2. Pinga, or industrial Cachaça is a common alcohol in the slums (favelas) of Brazil.

some notes for dancing
some measures for catching breath
some endings left hanging
some beginnings never begun
lunging baselines riddling the lungs
and everyone
just barely
breathing with them

I opened a poem
and there flew a song:
a round flash of lightening
without thunder and its sound
like a blink of blazing
in the fading of night,
the pitter-patter of quick light raindrops
on a rooftop just above you
and the splish-splash of quick light raindrops
on a rooftop just next to you

       In one arc of the wheel
       there are intricately changing sounds
       with bouts of boom and silence
       In another arc there is always
       only rain and storming

       *

a woman has no blouse
another blouseless woman
gives her duct tape for her torso

a migrant Midwest ranch-hand
makes a home which isn't really there
but another migrant ranch-hand knows
that they are both in it

on a day of cold rain
a brother has no transport
to go buy milk and cigarettes
so he places a cardboard box
over his baby sister's carriage
and like this, they make their way

an arthritic quadriplegic missing a finger
honours each and every finger she has left
with 3 or 4 rings
of silver and stones

the humour in the Chinese saying
that the dams on the Yangtze River are all made of tofu–
to deal with the harshness
of frequent floods

>   Lacking what we lack, all there is to do is give—
>   in one arc of the wheel there is utter emptiness,
>   in another arc, brimming depth

>   *

To open our gates
and wait with that openness
to greet what comes
and what we come to

Such stillness requires calm movement
spreading the weight of this waiting
as evenly as possible:

when the trees were bushy
they saw the trees, thick and textured leafy
when the trees were dropping leaves
they saw a mat of mustard-bronze-red

extending from tips of branches
to wheels parked at the tip of a lot in front
when the trees were bare
they saw through to the river, still with milky-ice
in the split moment before Spring
ice having broken to chunks, trees as yet unbudded
they saw the river – lustrous, flowing

>These were people who couldn't move
>from the front window
>Still, they saw so much.

What
is vulnerability
but the weight of patience
waiting in active stillness,
wandering with calm movement
for all that we may find.
And pain, the ultimate patience
the pain that we risk
in opening ourselves,
in giving

>It stretches us more porous if we let it.

*

To make love the lump in our throats.

The poem, an abstraction
The song, a soaring secret:
gull of a grand world
at peace with the still self
and one with the bare
bareness of being.

Memorial of the King of Lukembe, 2013

—for Achilla Araa Opuu-Idomo

First a griot chanting
Greeting-prayer-opening
In a language unknown to Achilla
and most of us
But understood via pitch

A tribute in white
Flowing white cloth
Bowls of white powder
Bright white to celebrate
The bright light of Achilla
eyes, heart and sounds

'I don't belong to you
You don't belong to me
We are together'
First of several choruses
Sung for Achilla

'It is a sad honour, a big honour
To sing for Achilla'
Subway musician who met
Achilla, the subway musician
Crossing many rivers in
the Toronto subway

Njacko Backo playing

Kula—Voice of the Spirit
On kalimba (lukembe)
'The little instrument that took
Achilla around the world.'

The MC speaking for all of us:
'We would like to honour Achilla's wife
Just arrived from Uganda, and here with us today
Achilla's former partner and
Achilla's son
Achilla was our friend
So you are our friends'

And Ruth Mathiang
Singing the love song of East Africa
and all the angels in the room
Singing along

'apoeme ate apeome ata'
Thank you for being, thank you for being you
Achilla's greeting
Each time he called

'wo ye wo kwenda mbire'
Safe journey from this place
To where you are going
Shona song sung to mbira (lukembe-in-a-bowl)

Anjoli
Song sung by Banaa Afrique
Song Achilla liked to open concerts with
'It took two people tonight to do what Achilla did
One on lukembe, one singing'

And the African Guitar Summit
Playing one short

But the entire Lula Lounge
Dancing in that spirit
Transcending all languages
Larger than us all.

Early Morning Train

Waking in morning dark
To catch you
the air is so quiet
even in this world city
I can hear towel brushing with skin
as it dries showered body.

Riding to the station
where I'll find you
there's a poem in the subway
about the preciousness of coffee
giving courage to wake up to the world.

Walking onto you
with the same backpack I had
the last time I took a train
I recall the journey before:
to flavours beyond taste buds
clouds larger than sky
and a kiss – deep and fleeting
as weed.

I thank you, Early Morning Train
for another chance to expand:
new stations to become acquainted with
unfamiliar smiles to crack
wildflowers of a strain I have never seen
novel things to come into, say hello and goodbye to.

Early Morning Train

You give me the courage to wake up to the world
By moving me on a track right through it.

Cartography of faith

Flying further west
while you are further east
I feel myself
nearing you somehow
as I begin nearing
the place you will be nearing
two weeks from now.
But even if you weren't
to be joining me there so soon
I know that west and east
always meet
so long as there's movement
and stillness too
In this I have the cartographers' faith
But faith
such a challenge
Will you etch-out this map with me?
Inlay it with
the movement of approaching
the stillness of meeting
Only to fly together
some time
some place
faithfully soon.

Kalisthenics of Displacement

to journey
in search of the past
is to find
all manner of things:
the traceable past
the past dispossessed
the past stood still
the past archived
the past historicised: planted to grow

                                                into a future

the past turned to art:
to release pain without acquitting it
the past lost
the past moving to sounds of the present

to journey
in search of the past
is an exercise
of
the needy
the curious
the restless
those who have journeyed so far
that displacement
opens questions
of every past

        every future
        all presents.

the present
is little other
than a cycle of futures passed
each present named 'new'
a window:
the past revealing itself
to under-journeyed namers

Circumventing Circumcisions

Her lips were tight
Never parting
too wide
for too many words
or too wide a kiss
"If you are sex-y"
she said
"they can never de-sex you"
Her lips
plum-full
But pursed.

Because of the migration
she could now
spare her daughter
the ritual
Her daughter:
lips free
legs fast
eyes wide
speaking early
in many tongues.
But she felt
she could not
shepherd
her daughter
the way her mother had shepherded her.

The migration
was mitigating

but left her ashore.
Her longings
had become foreign
Her life,
a stranger
How to phonate,
to be erect
in a new place
of different constraints?

Her mother arrived
another face,
another frame,
the wars back home intensifying.
Progeny and territory
Flesh and hunger
Meat and potatoes
Her mother cut,
she cooked,
her daughter consumed
persevering retreating resurging
the sepia-flow unsealable

You can't bleed the life from woman

a journalist at war
trapped in a hole
for 27 days

a town that inquires
how and why
a gay town member
21 thin years
was picked up by 2 town members
driven far
thrashed, rolled in snow, rapped on wire
left hanging

a migrant worker
returning home after 13 years
(deported for birthing a union)
to find a 13 year old daughter
who looks just like him
but can't accept his face

a man and a woman
both 40
both militants in a reactionary age
— I am 40 and I have nothing
— We are 40 and what we have
is all that we have fought for
and won
and lost.

                                          pushed to the edge
                                              here, a cliff

steep but more flush
than the rocks over there

because a soft grounding
is nowhere in sight
there is nothing to choose
but the

leap of hope

Wind

can't admit
you're caged by a monster offering wings
so wrapped in flight are you

you are what's behind
the light behind
the thick green glass

but your guitar strings
are strums
stretching further than those singing in
the air between loud bouncing strings

this time you've uprooted and displaced yourself
twice in one breath

like Robert Hedin's rapeseed and sunflowers
revolting against their rows, testing their souls
in the festival of the wind[1]
you feel detached like never before
Rebelling against your choices
as soon as you make them.

---

1. From Robert Hedin's poem 'Transcanadian', in *Snow Country* (Copper Canyon Press: 1975)

Toronto, 2004

Spent my last morning in that city
with two women from across the street
—a Mexican and her daughter—
at a street sale organised
by a woman from around the corner
of South Asian descent
Had lived there two years
but here was the first time
I was meeting any of them.

During the sale I invited
the Señora's daughter
(avoiding to speak her mother tongue
in front of me)
to browse through the clothes
I was selling on their lawn.
Liking two pieces, she chose one and asked the price
I told her to go ahead and take it.

Near the end of the rare gathering
I gave the daughter
the second piece of clothing.
Later her mum asked her to give me
the four Mexican mugs
I had eyed on their table.

here was Toronto's first gift to me

Letter to us via Reetika Vazirani

Toronto, March 2004

They taught us
volunteers
running Suicide Action Montréal
That a caller's
"I want to kill myself"
should always be taken
seriously
And followed up
with the question
"How do you plan on doing it?"
If an answer
full
of methodic steps
came up
we were told to
rate the call
on the urgent side of
the numeric scale and
act accordingly.
The failing
I felt
every
time
as an anonymous stranger
on the other end
of the line:
I wasn't permitted
to find

and meet
the caller
I had to have the call
traced
Maintain the
anonymous distance
Send a ticket to a
mental health ward
instead of unconditional support
to another human being
crying out
for help.

Dear Reetika Vazirani,
I never spoke
anonymously
with you.
You were averse
to suicide hotlines
to the ambulances
they'd send and
the hospitals
they'd send you to.
In any case we weren't in the same
cities
Not even
the same
country
for the most part
Still
somehow
somewhere
as a poet
as a woman
as a reader of the first Press

to publish you[1]
as some sort of South Asian in
North America
as an anonymous stranger
I know you.

Dear Reetika Vazirani,
This isn't a poem for you
You are long gone
Stabbed to death
along with your son
by a kitchen knife
in your hand.
Eight months after your death,
following an inexplicably long
Feature[2]
What are we
to make of your story?
Dear Reetika Vazirani
This is not an homage to you.
This is a letter to us
To better understand ourselves
To better understand the place that you left.

You picked poetry as
your trade
(different from poetry
as hobby)
A near-impossible choice

---

1. Copper Canyon Press—a 46-year-old, non-profit, unique publisher of poetry published Reetika Vazirani's second collection of poems, *World Hotel*, in 2002 (see www.coppercanyonpress.org). Her first collection, *White Elephants*, was awarded the Barnard New Women Poets Prize in 1996 and was published as part of the award.
2. See 'The Failing Light', by Paula Span, *Washington Post Magazine*, February 15, 2004.

for the daughter of professional Indian immigrants
driven by the pursuits
of both
Knowledge and Social Acknowledgment
(your father
an Assistant Dean and
oral surgeon
concurrently).
A near-impossible choice
because much like the
insightful
short films
I went to see
the other day
offered by the
Art Film House
for absolutely
free
Next to nobody
wants poetry.
And the supply
is so much greater than
the demand
And those who acknowledge it
are so few and far between
"those who have been forced
to a knowledge that has
severed knowing
into the smallest pieces"
as Susan Griffin puts it,
"fragments flying into
the far corners of a fractured world."[3]

3. From Susan Griffin's poem, 'To the Far Corners of Fractured Worlds', in her *Collected Poems* (Copper Canyon Press, 1997).

Dear Reetika Vazirani,
You fell in deep love
with a poet you didn't know
for long.
For fragments flying in a
fractured world
this makes sense.
As a poet he was in touch
with a touch
you could also touch
This came through
in the dancing rhythm
you shared
in the creative child
laid bare
by the fruit of your love
which rotted.
Dear Reetika Vazirani
All this makes perfect sense
to the far corners of fractured worlds
My deepest fall
in love
was with the mystery of a face
which had never
locked eyes
with another:
A poet
I knew briefly
but overlapped with
intensely
and then had to leave
for our joint safety.

Dear Reetika Vazirani,
Your lover was a

black male poet
of no uncertain acclaim.
Of course, such acclaim
was more possible for him:
Male in a
Black and White Nation
whose poetic vision
would be that much more accessible
because his male and black history
is that much more familiar
than female and red
or female and brown
or female and blue.
But when your poet-lover's acclaim
transferred some
concrete recognition
to you
It all became too real,
the reality of your place:
a lesser-known poet
(published, yes. award-winning, yes)
who bore the child of a better-known poet
and through this
gained
the long sought
acknowledgement-cum-opportunity
of a financially significant
'poetry-job'
(with the potential of becoming permanent)
A Lesser-Known Female Poet
gaining some significant
social space
which was not significant enough
because it wasn't all that significant

as the carry-on of
Black Male Acclaim.

And you had so very much to give,
Dear Reetika Vazirani.
words
ideas
gests
and other things appropriate.
Agile as you were
you could easily fit
in
but always
as a white elephant
roaming world hotels
And so, it was not easy
to know you fully.
Your colleagues and friends
saw your joy and
flair of giving
and believed this to be happiness.
What you didn't have
perhaps
was the sufficient presence of others
within which to give
all you had to give.
It wasn't sensed,
all that you had to offer
And so, much remained
un-taken
And in this way we didn't accept
you
Dear Reetika Vazirani
And that is where
you were alone.

And that is where we didn't look
beneath
the surfaces
we didn't look close enough
And so we didn't do
enough
And that is where
we can always
do better.

Dear Reetika Vazirani,
You took your toddler son
with you.
An affront to National Family Values
In a nation where suicide
takes more deaths than
homicide
And some 1000 traced cases
of mothers killing their children
in the past 10 US years
show mothers usually killing
themselves
as well.
"purposeful filicide"
There is purpose there
Where women don't want to
abandon their children
don't want their children
to grow up without Mum
And for you, Reetika Vazirani
first alone in your isolation,
then alone in your isolation x2
It followed
for you
and your son

to go together.
Alone together
Dead together.

And then there were
the anti-depressants and therapists
that your loved ones knew of
Dear Reetika Vazirani.
Some internal imbalance
chemical or otherwise
rendered or genetic
(there was also your father's suicide)
Or all of the above
Who knows?
Maybe the final trials you endured:
Love Motherhood Success
pushed you past
the threshold
Suicide and Filicide
flowing from
a National Internal Imbalance
gone-out-of-whack.

Dear Reetika Vazirani,
There were chronic callers
at Suicide Action Montréal.
Mostly sufferers of
internal imbalances
with no one else to reach
for.
They called often
contemplated suicide
often
and attempted suicide
more than once.

Sometimes with success
These chronic cases
we were told
were calls not to waste long with
Because time is short
and hotline volunteers
are few
and the suicides are many
and there is no way to know for sure
when a chronic caller
is about to self-kill
and there was a lack of statistics
on this
And for all these reasons
these cases
were worth less
in the non-profit business
of suicide hotlines

But you made chronic calls
for help
to friends
Dear Reetika Vazirani:

the 12 page list of detailed instructions
to be followed after your death
(left among a friend's files)

the emergency need to flee an unsafe place
in your lover's house
(group-emailed to friends)

several statements to friends about feeling
unsafe

"Sometimes I think it would be easier

to do what my father did and just go to sleep"
to a friend on the phone

the July 16, 7:15am call to a friend
Announcing your decision to hurt yourself and your son
who told you to call a suicide hotline[4]

Dear Reetika Vazirani
In a society of people
keeping distances
from all but those
immediately involved
in their lives
An entire Suicide Action Industry
(even publicly-funded therapy)
can do little
to unbind
our alienation from each other
(even in Canada we have plenty of suicides).
Dear Reetika Vazirani
Here
Now
I commit
to not keeping
polite
or safe distances.

Dear Reetika Vazirani,
It's late in the city
and you are asleep.[5]
This isn't a message for you
Just a stranger's attempt

4. Reetika Vazirani and her son, Jehan Vazirani Komunyakaa, were found dead in the afternoon of July 16, 2003.
5. This stanza echoes Reetika Vazirani's poem 'It's Me, I'm Not Home', from *World Hotel* (Copper Canyon Press: 2002).

to enter
         without romance
a familiar map of homelessness
To pick up the receiver
And try to make something
of the key you left.

On love XXIII

looking for the woman beneath the skin
Incipient and wandering
she is somewhere between
the woman outside
and the woman within

Playing by ear
Sketching with the wind
Tapping into scents
Walking into the woman beneath the skin

tall and small
wide and thin
Ripples and crashing
she is the river and the sea
breathing within

Embracing what she doesn't have
not settling for what she can
Reframing the possibilities of
fusing the world with the woman within

long locks and waves
curls and shaves
Braided up and rooted in
she is the hair around the nipples
and the hair she feels the need to trim

Anticipating and waiting
for the woman outside

She's making latent love
with the woman within.

Last Note to a Brother-Comrade

Feels like parts of me
have been left behind
in each of the places I've been

I want to make something new
right here with you
Do you want to make it with me

From chant to article to
letter to update
We met and parted
and met again—
How many more rallies and
campaigns and wordy encounters
'til I come to know you

                     the igniting, ongoing, as we make a go of it

To feel is to plunge deep
into the tragedy of joy:
to taste joy and then
to face it in its briefness
Joy so clever in its way
of making us want it
never to cease

                     the struggle is what's ceaseless

To express a feeling
is to cast one's tragedy and joys
into the imagery of another

And to coast or be caught
in that strangeness

I want to feel you
and you, me
in a strangeness strange to us both
like ghosts in self-revolt

I want to make something new with you
Do you want to make it with me

Clifton Sunset

Inspiring
like the life-loving laughter
of a fully-clad 'Black' man
running into the sun
along a ridged wall
edging a cliff
hanging over the ocean
At sunset.[1]

---

[1] To this day, Clifton is an all-'White' neighbourhood in a highly-constructed, beautiful, wealthy part of Cape Town.

Bleeding Heart, or Toronto 2016

two bunnies
you opened your doors
we leaped in, opened further

a pair of ice skates gliding us together:
poetry, piano, politics

a bottle of wine
(or two or three)
dinner in the garden and
cooking frozen cherries like never before

the harp, a rendering of the kora
its strings the sounds of receiving and giving
It sings today of grace
the song we hear thinking of you.

---

1. Bleeding Heart: A flower which can be pulled apart into two rabbits, two old fashioned ice skates, a bottle of wine and a harp.

On Methodology

—to Ronald Gonzalez (Binghamton)

Some started with much
and gradually trimmed and shaped
with a box tool and finger scissors
Some built minimally, first coating the wire thinly with clay
then successively layering
Some made the block platform,
upon which sat the stool
upon which sat the body
Some used a brick or two instead of making the block and stool
Some built stool legs and sculpted up from there
Some sculpted the body from feet dangling in air
Some sculpted the body from feet touching a surface

Some formed the cone with a sheet of clay fashioned from lumps
flattened in hands
then wrapped around the body like a cape,
leaving space in between: "felt space"
felt
by the sculptor
or the body
or both
Some composed the body and cone as if they were one,
the cone full of something more
than only body or clay

Is the whole more than the sum of the parts
Is the sum of parts even more than that whole

Does this summing actually produce a multiple
Are some parts more than the entire whole
Are the parts and whole factors of something yet more?

Some made the cone-hat and plonked it on the head
Some shaped the cone-hat and the head simultaneously
Some scraped lines between head and shoulders: hair
Some smacked clay into a plaque
and shaped it into hair over a cone-less scull
Some sculpted faces and nothing but detailed faces

What
was there?

Through the cones we can know some
through the stool we can know some
through the body we can know some
through the block we can know some

They were all there:
wavelengths of different frequencies
posited and abstracted for sculpting here.

The sculptors and the sculpted:
parts of a texture-enmeshing flux
as knowing as lost as unknowing as unknown
as one another
But always, still
sculpting
something.

the first thing that stood out
Not the necklaces crossing
your neck and chest
Not the anklets of clay bells
Not the knee brace
Not the beads
roped
1000 times around your wrists
Not the white powder covering you in
intentional patches
Not your red and white chokers
Not your breasts with penis
But the cowry-beaded mohawk braid trailing
and cowry-studded sideburns framing
Precious shells of Mapungubwe
re-emerging in your
Closet Chant

    —to Albert Ibokwe (Johannesburg)

Liberation

In my path these mornings:

firefly wings

limp leaves of gooseberry bush
no longer sheltering budding fruit

Chose a film about a ghost
helping another ghost move on
The only answer:
ghosts have ghosts too
Ghosts from life
following ghosts that have passed

In this expansive journey
it's as though I am flying
to and from death simultaneously
Like how I am leaving
one daughter behind
only to find another on landing
Or how
human helplessness
is the mystery
of both
life and death

Maulana Rumi says

                    The way of love is not
                    a subtle argument

                        The door there
                        is devastation

I say

Generosity is the room we enter

stubby, star shaped tufts of carrot-seed grass
sprouting, then shedding on impoverished soil
Making way in time for feathery stalks of sweet grass

wings de-winged and liberated.

www.ingramcontent.com/pod-product-compliance
Lightning Source LLC
Chambersburg PA
CBHW050540300426
44113CB00012B/2190